DOROTHY LEIGH SAYERS AND THE FENS

Trevor Bevis

WITH AN ACCOUNT OF HER NOVEL, THE NINE TAILORS, BASED ON THE CAMBRIDGESHIRE FENS

GW00578144

PUBLISHED BY TREVOR BEVIS BA, 28 ST. PETER'S ROAD, MARCH, CAMBS.
Tel: 01354 657286

PRINTED BY DAVID J. RICHARDS, 1 WEST PARK STREET, CHATTERIS, CAMBS.
Tel: 01354 692947   Fax: 01354 692299

DOROTHY LEIGH SAYERS AND THE FENS

The substantial "flood tower" at Terrington St. Clement. In ancient times parishioners took refuge in the tower when sea embankments gave way. Boats from King's Lynn carried essential supplies to the occupants. The structure is slightly detached from the church for fear of its weight unsettling the building. Eight bells were used for the BBC's film The Nine Tailors.

Dorothy L. Sayers

Possessed zeal to understand the Fens' great history

DOROTHY L. SAYERS

Dorothy Leigh Sayers was born on June 13th 1893 at Oxford where her father the Reverend Henry Sayers was headmaster at Christchurch Choir School. An only child she was brought up at Bluntisham rectory, Cambridgeshire and went on to Godolphin School, Salisbury, there winning a scholarship to Somerville College, Oxford. She graduated in 1915 with a first class honours degree in modern languages. Academic life was not entirely to her liking and she found work at Blackwell's, a firm of Oxford publishers, worked with a friend Eric Whelpton at L'Ecole des Roches in Normandy and served as a copywriter at the London advertising firm of Bensons from 1922 until 1931.

Displaying rare imaginative talent her earliest publications in verse were *Op I* (1916) and *Catholic Tales* (1918). Blessed with a keen analytical mind with inbred skill of a wordsmith she determined to earn a living by writing detective stories, a decision which earned her the accolade of being the greatest detective writer in the golden age of mystery thrillers. She was a scholar in mediaeval studies as well as a profound religious thinker and characteristically mastered the craft of writing, well perceived in her accomplished novels in particular *The Nine Tailors* which necessitated a close analytical study of the theory of the art of change ringing on bells. This novel, said to be the cunningest ever written, was set in the Fenland area of Cambridgeshire with which Dorothy was familiar.

One of the first women to obtain an Oxford degree, Dorothy benefitted considerably from her academic training and the ability to learn quickly. She adhered persistently to her own way of thinking and introduced a pleasant literary consistence to her unique manner of writing. She came close to blending the attractions of her style with the values of science fiction, a rare thing among authors, then not achieved since the days of Wilkie Collins. If a memorial exists to her it is embodied in her renowned detective stories masterfully concocted and established strongly, seriously and humorously upon her likeable character Lord Peter Wimsey, powerfully placed in a succession of mystery thrillers – *Whose Body* (1923), *Clouds Of Witness* (1926), *Unnatural Death* (1927), *Lord Peter Views The Body* (1928), *The Unpleasantness At The Bellona Club* (1928), *Strong Poison* (1930), *The Documents Of The Case* (1930), *The Five Red Herrings* and *Have His Carcase* (1932).

During her last few years as a writer of mystery novels Dorothy Sayers extended her range and produced *Murder Must Advertise* (1933), *The Nine Tailors* (1934) and *Gaudy Night* (1935). These played a major role in increasng the scope of her literary powers as an atmospheric writer as well as a writer of social comedy. The trend continued with *Busman's Honeymoon* (1937), a work which concluded the adventures of gentleman detective Lord Peter. Busman's Honeymoon was successfully dramatised in collaboration with M. St. Clare Byrne.

The demise of Lord Peter Wimsey and the highly successful detective series led Dorothy to another literary challenge, that of the Christian apologist. A sincere doctrinal Anglican she produced two plays for the Canterbury Festival, *The Zeal Of Thy House* (1937) and *The Devil To Pay* (1939). Then followed *The Man Born To Be King* broadcast between December 1941 and October 1942. The war led her to write *Begin Here* and this was followed by *The Mind Of The Maker* in which she compares the human with the Divine Creator. Among her other works are *The Greatest Drama Ever Staged* (1950), *The Empress Constantine* (play, 1951), *Introductory Papers On Dante* (1954), *Further Papers On Dante* (1957), *The Song Of Roland* (1957), *The Days Of Christ's Coming* (1960) and *The Poetry Of Search And The Poetry Of Statement* (posthumous essays, 1963). Dorothy wrote several volumes containing studies, essays and speeches on critical, theological and political subjects. In 1950 Durham University presented her with an honorary D.Litt. This was followed in 1955 by her last but one publication *Purgatorio*.

All her writing life Dorothy penned numerous essays, letters and articles, often sitting up until the early hours. She was gifted with rare good humour and her wit and fine powers of concentration embued her with a formidable presence. She completed volumes on critical, theological and political subjects and relished strong, energetic debate adding spice to many circles with which she associated. Much in demand as a lecturer Dorothy performed sterling work at the St. Anne's Centre for Christian Discourse. She also found time to act as churchwarden of St. Thomas–cum–St. Anne's church, London. In 1928 she acquired a cottage at Witham, Essex for her widowed mother and following Mrs. Sayers death a short time later Dorothy purchased the house next door and had both properties made into one for her own use.

While working on *Paradiso* Dorothy became ill quite unexpectedly and died at her home on December 17th 1957. The manuscript was completed by her friend, Dr. Barbara Reynolds.

Dorothy Sayers married in 1926 Capt. Arthur Fleming, a war correspondent.

Fenny scene

The Fen landscape and rivers embued Dorothy Sayers with a sense
of great happenings and stoic independence

FEN BACKCLOTH

Acknowledged for her ability to dissect in depth subjects pertaining to her literary skills, Dorothy Sayers quickly discovered that the Cambridgeshre Fens harboured more in its vast acreage of high yielding fields and orchards than flatness of landscape suggests. "The Nation's Breadbasket", "Holy Land of the English" and "Land of the Three-quarter Sky" prescribes in part the Fen's epic past. Many are its famous and infamous names involved with lost and just causes strident through English history.

This historically famous region, the haunt of anglers and botanists, offered final sanctuary to the Anglo-Saxon race led by Hereward the Wake. The Fens were the early marching grounds of its most famous son, Oliver Cromwell, and the flatland earned an envious reputation by many other means. A land of matchless skies, sunrises and sunsets, of wide horizons, partly beneath sea level protected by earth barriers and a complex drainage system which saved it from total inundation time and time again.

Great changes have taken place in the past three-and-a-half centuries from the time of Sir Cornelius Vermuyden, eminent Dutch land drainage expert who designed the first "impossible" scheme to drain water from the marsh and confine it to a myriad of rivers and drains. Errors of judgement occurred and during the past hundred years water coursing at a higher level than the shrinking soil spilled out from breached embankments and reclaimed its former domain devastating human lives, land, property and beast. Stoic Fen dwellers repeatedly fought back and won.

Not surprisingly the splendid isolation of watery waste obscured by writhing mist relieved anciently by islands here and there attracted recluse souls and Saxon tribes. Magnificent Norman cathedrals at Ely and Peterborough testify most nobly to the ancient Church with flamboyant influence exemplified in well-known monastic ruins at Crowland, Thorney, Ramsey and other places.

There are numerous examples of exceptional churches stretching in a broad arc within a twelve-mile distance inland from the Wash coastline between Boston and King's Lynn, predominantly a silt area. Other fine churches are set upon the low islands overlooking the peat fens which they anciently dominated. Spires and pinnacles thrust skywards as if vying with oneanother for best prominence. Mediaeval designers and craftsmen visualised the churches and steeples in particular as inspiring foils against a dead flat backcloth void of trees. In the marshland near the sea most churches with multi-staged towers were used as places of refuge by families besieged by floods. Some incorporate chambers with that in mind.

The Fens and Marshland are blessed with one of the finest groups of churches in Britain. Think of Walpole St. Peter, West Walton, Holbeach, Gedney, Moulton, Whaplode, Sutton-in-the-Isle, Leverington, Whittlesey, Wisbech and Tydd St. Giles. In addition there are the three special Sayers churches, Terrington St. Clement, Upwell and St. Wendreda's at March. These inspired Dorothy Sayers for her novel *The Nine Tailors*. At all these places the mind is tantalised by the best in traditional ecclesiastical craftsmanship. Some Marshland churches differ to those elsewhere in the country because they were erected with the flooded landscape in mind, so much a part of the mediaeval fen dwellers traumatic lives.

The Sayers family was well read in quintessential elements such as these. Dorothy admirably portrayed her perceptive skills and obvious knowledge of the Fens in her special, very popular literary achievement. *The Nine Tailors* is a near perfect reflection of the Fens and what happened in geological terms centuries ago and even in living memory.

DOMES, SPIRES AND FEN

When the Sayers family came to the Fens, for the Reverend Henry, a classical scholar and adept musician, the geological aspect could not have been more different. He had accepted the living at Bluntisham, a small Huntingdonshire village on the edge of the Fens, now owing to boundary changes included in Cambridgeshire. To the south of Bluntisham ranges undulating countryside not unlike Oxfordshire, punctuated with woods and to the north low rolling meadows merge starkly with endless acres of grain-yielding fields intersected by a myriad of dykes and artificial drains of startling conformity. The move was a dramatic change to what Henry Sayers had been used to.

Helen Mary Sayers was delivered of her daughter, Dorothy on June 13th 1893 at Oxford, city of dreaming towers and domes, the centre of academic elite. Her husband, educated at Magdalen College, was later appointed headmaster at Christchurch cathedral choir school, an eminently suitable post for a gifted musician and theologian. The family, including Dorothy's grandmother and maiden aunt, lived in a cramped house and that was partly the reason for the move to the countryside. At an early age Dorothy was known to be noisy and boisterous, embued with great curiosity and displayed the hallmarks of intelligence.

The move to Bluntisham was preceded by a great deal of preparation and the family anticipated the change with much enthusiasm. At Bluntisham, the rectory, a large rambling old house in the finest rural Georgian tradition was situated some distance from the striking mediaeval church with its triangular apse said to be unique in England. Unquestionably a fine building with a handsome tower surmounted with a spire having no fewer than twelve small windows, the church occupied a lasting place in Henry Sayers heart and his appreciation for the Gothic style knew no bounds. He was soon at home in his new surroundings. His love for liturgical expression developed at Oxford and this naturally enveloped his family including the observant young Dorothy who, in later life, reflected her father's perceptiveness in these matters.

The Sayers new home was exactly the opposite of their restricted house at Oxford. At Bluntisham there were rooms galore including ample accommodation for servants. When the family arrived at the village they found that life revolved around agriculture and seasonal wildfowling, rivers nearby spilling into meadows designed to take the brunt of winter's rising water levels. It afforded ideal conditions for water sports including that Fen speciality, speed skating.

The church as always was at the centre of village life and played a large part in local events in which Mrs. Sayers took part. Dorothy, at the forefront of things, was equally keen to be involved. Her mother must have missed the social round at Oxford where the Reverend Sayers academical interests and position at Christchurch cathedral were in constant demand. As rector at Bluntisham his newfound lifestyle, while demanding in a different kind of way, allowed a less hasty approach within his round of responsibilities.

"Thus the rector, an old-fashioned parson of the Broad Church type, was ably supported in the fulfilment of his pastoral responsibilities, which he managed, in a leisurely way, to combine with the life of a country gentleman". – (Barbara Reynolds: DOROTHY SAYERS, HER LIFE AND SOUL. Reproduced by permission of Hodder & Stoughton Limited).

Dorothy found plenty to do in her tender years at Bluntisham and showed interest in traditional fen skating, the stuff that champions are made of, a few famous names from the area successfully taking on the best that Scandinavia could offer. Learning to skate at nearby Earith with its twin rivers and intervening washland was, for Dorothy, a salutary introduction to the Fens, later to play a major role in her fame as an author. Inside the rectory Dorothy enjoyed happy hours in her nursery littered with playthings which she often affectionately recalled to mind.

She had the freedom of a substantial garden and enjoyed playing among the blooms in spring and summer months. A local gardener was employed and later his services were retained to attend to the rectory gardens at Christchurch. The Reverend Sayers worked from a study overlooking idyllic scenes of beautifully kept lawns and flower beds, flowering bushes and stately trees. He drew inspiration from the sound of song birds trilling among the leafy boughs, something the family lacked in the environs of their former home at Oxford.

A mile or two along the road from Bluntisham, Sir Cornelius Vermuyden's workmen, mainly Scottish and Dutch prisoners-of-war in 1650 commenced the ponderous task of excavating the New Bedford river. Dorothy was taken to the water meadows now and then and was probably intrigued by the ancient sconce – an earthwork from the English Civil War. Sometimes she sat in a trap drawn by a pony led by a village young man who had a good knowledge about local wild life. She displayed vivid imagination and a strong resolve with her boisterous attitude, perfect ingredients for a potential author. Her youthful memories of Bluntisham were happy ones, if a little lack lustre, and later in her life she and a friend took delight in visiting the village and meeting individuals she had known in her younger days.

Her opinion of the Fen country as dreary derived from her early impression of the flat countryside around Bluntisham canopied by an unforgiving three-quarter sky, this enhanced even more so from the stark fen surrounding the village of Christchurch. She later intimated she had never acquired a fondness of the Fens. Nevertheless Dorothy seems to have discovered, as do many, a rare sense of freedom in the Fens exemplified by the stoic and independent qualities of true Fenfolk whom she admired. She recognised a creative mystery threaded into the Fens' epic history which she obviously read. How otherwise would she have known about the floods of old? This knowledge is vividly portrayed in her novel *The Nine Tailors,* arguably her finest detective story.

The Old Rectory at Bluntisham. As a young girl Dorothy Sayers grew up amid idyllic scenery surrounding the house. Two miles away the Bedford Rivers began their parallel courses through the Fens. There, Dorothy was introduced to the wetlands and especially to the Fen tradition of speed skating.

When the Reverend Henry Sayers held the livings of Bluntisham and Christchurch few motor cars could be found in the Fens. Certainly land workers and farmers of small holdings could not afford them. To a large extent the motor car transformed the Fens and became an essential means of transport in this most rural of rural areas. Dorothy Sayers regarded cars as suitable only for genteel folk and she far preferred motor cycles!

Mechanised transport opened the highways and byways to the more adventurous minded and by the time Dorothy's parents left Bluntisham to live at Christchurch, the wealthier Fen inhabitants notably gentlemen farmers with motor cars frequently visited the upland regions, cities and seaside resorts, something their waterborne ancestors were unable to do.

Dorothy's academical traints saw her studying at Salisbury and Oxford where she gained an MA degree in languages. Growing older she developed her own ideas about religion and was unattracted to simplistic evangelical methods. Her fervour surfaced in admiration and love of scriptural language unchanged in the centuries. The rhythm and beauty of biblical passages of the old order to her way of thinking surpassed by far the starkness of modern scriptural language. It was a first impression of a potential writer. Undoubtedly this reflected from her father who impressed his daughter with desirability of the Benedictine approach and harmonising splendour of noble Gothic aspiration combining as a whole in the glorification of God.

Dorothy enjoyed meeting people and delighted in an academic circle of friends. One, a chaplain at Oxford, titillated her feelings for male company. The young man's winning manner and finely chiselled features later created in Dorothy's mind the base model for her debonair sleuth Lord Peter Wimsey, the central figure in her renowned detective series.

St. Wendreda's church, March, is one of the three Sayers churches which provided Dorothy with inspiration for Fenchurch St. Paul, the centrepiece for her novel The Nine Tailors. The bells, cast from the metal of mediaeval and seventeenth century bells, are a fine ring of six by Thomas Osborn of Downham Market in 1802. They were brought to March on a barge via the Fenland river system.

The stunning early 16th century double-hammerbeam angel ceiling viewed from the ringing gallery at St. Wendreda's church, March. In Dorothy Sayers novel, Mrs. Venables, conducting Lord Peter Wimsey around Fenchurch St. Paul's remarks in her opinion the roof is finer than those at March and Needham Market.

"THE LAST PLACE THAT GOD MADE . . .

. . . and he forgot the staircase" was how Dorothy Sayers described Christchurch, Cambridgeshire. At Bluntisham, the close proximity of Huntingdonshire's undulating countryside carresses the eye with pleasing if distant vistas. In defining a typical Fen village slap-bang in the middle of nowhere, literally as flat as the proverbial pancake, one might point out Christchurch as the likely place. Set in a vast plain, bounded on every side by wheat fields and long rows of sugar beet and potatoes growing bountifully where water once reigned supreme, Christchurch is a relatively small village which had its beginnings from the great drainage scheme begun more than three centuries ago. Water, oceans of it, is still the Fens' foremost element but nowadays it is confined to dead-straight, deep drains – the burial places of many old cars – controlled by numerous manned and automatic pumps with a giant sluice here and there to protect reclaimed land from tidal surge.

Christchurch was included in the old Isle of Ely of historic fame, an area of semi-religious association with the offices of the Bishop of Ely, similar to Co. Durham where the Prince Bishops held sway and even Kings had to seek permission to enter or cross the territory. Christchurch was known as Brimstone Hill supposedly derived from legendary source to the effect that the devil was driven out of Upwell to this isolated spot where he vented his fury and kept the local Fenmen on their toes! No obvious hill is to be seen and sulphurous fumes are agreeably absent! The village is almost hidden by a pleasant green canopy of venerable trees and has a long street adjoining another at a T-junction. It is, in fact, a peaceful, pretty little place and since the time Dorothy Sayers walked here, with the exception of new residences little seems to have changed. One of two public houses, The Dun Cow, certainly echoed to the laughter of Dorothy and her husband on the occasions they visited the village.

Henry Sayers' move to Christchurch in 1917 was a little unorthodox, the previous owner, Reverend Neville, who had a big family, desirous of vacating the parish for larger accommodation. He had his eye on Bluntisham with its commodious parsonage, ideal for family needs. Exchanging livings was uncommon and with the maxim in mind, "the end justifies the needs", Mr. Neville contacted Mr. Sayers and was surprised, one supposes, when the latter agreed to exchange. The stipend at Bluntisham was rosier, too, which makes it all the more astonishing that Henry Sayers agreed to the move, all the more so bearing in mind that, apart from his own immediate family, he had several resident relatives to support.

The Reverend and Mrs. Sayers were well respected by their new parishioners and he practised a charitable disposition to his new-found flock which numbered well less than a thousand souls. Most were employed full-time and some, mainly women, on a part-time seasonal basis on the land. Cycles were much in evidence and in those times teams of eight women cyclists – the "flying eights" – could be seen in long skirts and bonnets travelling miles in all weather conditions, to pick potatoes and single beet for local farmers. They were hardy individuals and were more than a match for men. They were a match, too, for the "drowning" seasons when implements were bogged down in the fields and the women donned wellingtons and persisted pluckily at their work. When the dreaded "fen blows" occurred forcing drivers to switch on headlights, they scornfully spat the dust from their mouths and turned their backs against the howling wind while topsoil and seeds, even roots, flew past them, and were resown in the back gardens of towns miles away. The Sayers family had inherited a parish of uncommon challenge.

The little red-brick church was a bit of a come-down for a man who liked to enthuse over the glories of mediaeval architecture. In no way can Christchurch's fane compare with that at Bluntisham, enriched with the tantalising niceties of adornment where spiritual values absorbed over the centuries

11

can be felt, a peculiarity existing in most ancient churches. Built in 1862 with short transepts the fane at Christchurch is a comely, welcoming building. Its dignity was more pronounced when it had its tower. This was pulled down soon after its completion, the weight disturbing foundations and causing cracks to appear along the south aisle. The church must have shrieked with ignominy when demolishers stopped by and the village lost its landmark seen for miles away in the Fens. The only thing saved was the bell which ting-tangs from the insignificant turret capped with a little spire. Victorians frequently made the mistake of laying foundations of insufficent strength in the Fens. Twisting clay did the rest as was certainly the case at Benwick where first the tower then the church was demolished. At Friday Bridge the tower's tell-tale lean offers the same story. Undoubtedly Henry Sayers and his daughter learned in their travels from one church to another there exists several Pisa's in the Fens, the king of the bunch undoubtedly that at Surfleet.

At the time that the Sayers moved to Christchurch Dorothy was putting the finishing touches to her teaching vocation at Hull. She returned to Oxford and found employment at Basil Blackwell's, taking leave occasionally to visit her parents. Eventually she went to France and was employed for a year at L'Eide des Roches, Verneuil. Returning to England Dorothy decided to take up employment in London and in August and September 1921 went to live with her parents at Christchurch. Anyone visiting the rectory which is privately owned, see it much as Dorothy remembered it.

With the Sayers family in mind, the writer has often wandered around the village, savoured cider at The Dun Cow and walked along a nearby drove in the footsteps of the novelist. Next to the church, flanked by venerable trees stands the gabled rectory where the family lived. What idleness the Victorian parsons had with servants to hand performing the daily round of domestic tasks. Apart from preparing notes for sermons they found plenty of time studying local history and writing books, visiting parishioners and supping tea in local homes. The Reverend Sayers, a conservative man by all accounts, discovered that the Great War changed the map of Victorian ideals but he was sufficiently flexible to "fit in". The isolated Fens was one of the last bastions of the old order to accept change and his inherited ways of the old school were allowed to infiltrate the new at a leisurely pace. One of Dorothy's friends, Eric Whelpton, who had worked with her abroad, visited Christchurch and was introduced to Henry and Mrs. Sayers. They found him likeable and attentive and he was impressed with the atmosphere of the typical Victorian country house and the charm of his hosts. This extended to the Sayers superb organisational abilities and splendid meals.

Christchurch rectory fell far short of the mansion-like granduer of that at Bluntisham. Nevertheless it was cosier for the Sayers with fewer rooms and offered comfortable accommodation. As at Bluntisham the garden area was extensive and Henry Sayers had the good fortune to employ the gardener who had served him at his former living. In recent years Christchurch rectory became a retreat known as Masters and shared its homeliness with all that savoured tranquility, good food and a amiable atmosphere. An oasis in the flatland where one betook oneself to bathe contemplatively in the all-enveloping atmosphere of good things. Here visitors re-assessed themselves and in the mornings awoke to the tantalising whiff of fried bacon drifting upstairs. That was the experience of Dorothy Sayers during her visits to Christchurch and it can be contemplated that these homely habits frequented her mind in the planning of *The Nine Tailors*, the Reverend Theodore Venables of Fenchurch St. Paul reflective of the charming manner of her beloved father. From the rectory windows she could look out above the wide expanse of fen canopied by the overwhelming sky like no other scene in Britain and, distantly, the grey, soaring bulk of Ely cathedral, ship of the Fens, silhouetted against the iridescent glow of changing cloudscape.

Dorothy had her own sitting room at the rectory and there she spent long hours making plans. Memories of the Fens' snow covered fields and rising embankments, the rivers waiting for half a chance to spill over undoubtedly inspired her when she planned *The Nine Tailors*. Unquestionably a fine novel the book possesses evocative connections with the Fens and is a masterpiece in its way.

Dorothy was a bookworm and seldom relaxed without a copy of the printed word resting on her knees. In her room with its unhindered, panoramic outlook over the great level in perfect quiet she added to her knowledge by reading good books. Dorothy admired great writers and her bedsitter was graced with several volumes by distinguished authors. Among them were copies of her earliest, if modest, non-fictional works printed during the First World War.

Already her interest in crime fiction had become apparent and she studied volumes relative to the subject, i.e. creation of the plot and the best techniques in writing it. Classics, too, occupied her interest and helped to develop her style, very important to potential authors who share with artists the necessity of personal uniqueness, on the one hand portraying the image of colour and shape by brush strokes and on the other hand expertly rendering a stylised mark with the use of words and pen. It was at Christchurch rectory in 1923 Dorothy applied final flourishes to her first Lord Peter novel *Whose Body*, and this, with her second literary offering *Clouds Of Witness* published in 1926, set her firmly in the direction of becoming a popular and internationally acclaimed novelist. Dorothy spent a lot of time in London and it was there that *Clouds Of Witness* was mostly written. She later completed it in Yorkshire, the background to the story.

Dorothy's early years as a writer were worrying and frustrating, this mainly due to delays and limited sources of income. It was her strongest wish to leave the teaching profession and earn a living from her finely honed powers of imagination and writing skills. This could not have been achieved without the patience and help of her father. To supplement her income she frequently travelled along the

14

raised embankment of the Sixteen Foot river which runs from near Chatteris to Upwell, and teach French on a part-time basis at the rectory, a noble, rambling old house with its beginnings in the 14th century. To approach the ancient church Dorothy had to pass through the turreted entrance of a 15th century curtain wall which once encircled the rectory gardens. The fine Perpendicular church impressed her to the extent that she used it and also two other Fen churches to inspire conception of her Fenchurch St. Paul in *The Nine Tailors*. Some of the ceilings are marvellously adorned with carvings of strange little creatures and she could examine some at close quarters from a Georgian gallery over the north aisle reached by a flight of steps. Of great curiosity the unusual gallery, to the writer's mind, detracts from the mediaeval interior.

The time spent at Christchurch subjected Dorothy to a period of anxiety and doubt. She stood at the crossroads, in one direction to continue her profession as a teacher with command of three languages; in the opposite direction a strong yearning to make progress in her desire to be an achieved author. Dorothy was foremost in her parents' mind and it seems she was none too happy working away. Nothing much outstanding was happening in her life and the Reverend and Mrs. Sayers did everything they could to comfort her: "They sent her fresh eggs from the country, and daffodils to decorate her room – once even some budding twigs. She sends her washing to save laundry bills. And she is trying hard to get a job". – (Barbara Reynolds: DOROTHY SAYERS, HER LIFE AND SOUL. Reproduced by permission of Hodder & Stoughton Limited).

For every potential author the urge to write is irresistible, and Dorothy was determined about her future. Part of her depression stemmed from the realisation that it is not easy to satisfy the demands of publishers who are exacting to a fine point and know precisely what is necessary to produce a good novel. Her heart was not in her teaching profession and the work barely kept her solvent. It was essential that she invent a central character for criminal fiction and write around him. In Lord Peter Wimsey she sensed a worthy vessel for a series

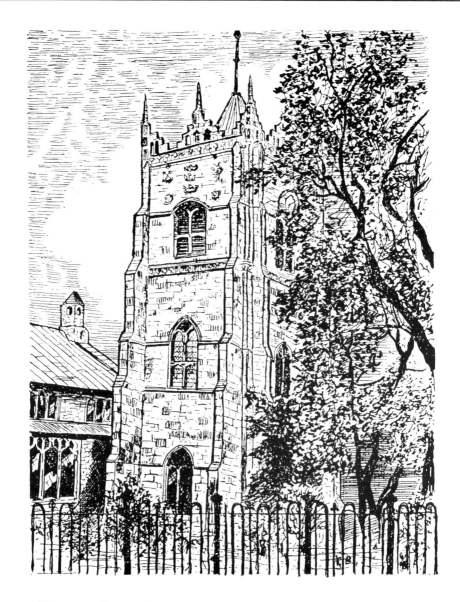

The commodious 16th century tower of St. Peter and St. Paul, Wisbech, was surely observed by Dorothy Sayers when she lived at Christchurch, a few miles away. Containing a tuneful ring of ten bells, the tower is embellished with coats of arms and various decorative devices. Dorothy used Wisbech and Walsoken for "Walbeach" in her internationally famous novel.

and was right in her assumption. Still assailed by doubt Dorothy was coming round to the conviction that inbred intuition and talent must in the end prevail.

Whose Body was dogged by delays. The manuscript had to be assessed and Dorothy's patience gave out prompting her to find another agent who was interested. Sensing a potential good seller he contacted an American publishing company which shared his instincts and consequently Dorothy was made an offer. Her prime aim was to break into the difficult arena as a novelist, an ambition which so often proves to be an unsurmountable obstacle to many would-be authors. This was an apprehensive time for Dorothy and her trial was heightened when she brought a baby son into the world. Knowledge of this was discreetly kept from the Reverend and Mrs. Sayers but eventually they had to be told and although saddened, they came to terms with the situation and were generously disposed towards Dorothy, the child and its father.

*　　*　　*　　*　　*　　*

Until fairly recently memories of the Sayers family lingered with one or two Christchurch inhabitants. An elderly villager now deceased, informed the writer that she had been employed by the family at the rectory and she personally knew Dorothy who could frequently be seen striding in her inimitable manner along the village street, hair protected by a headscarf – "the country type" – on windy days. Dorothy was in the habit of visiting the village stores to purchase cigarettes (she was addicted to the weed) and smoked from a holder. Occasionally she purchased a tin of tobacco for her mother who, the writer was told, smoked a pipe indoors, in those times not unusual for a woman of the country type as one would think. Women smokers were accepted in elite social circles but for one to be seen smoking out of doors was regarded as scandalous. Fen women emulated their husbands and smoked pipes which was quite normal. What with Dorothy reflectively blowing smoke rings at the ceiling and her mother indulging in the sitting-room, the rectory must have reeked a bit.

16

At Christchurch Dorothy gave the impression of being a loner. She probably missed the company of intellectuals, something she had enjoyed at Salisbury and Oxford. Some villagers thought she was a bit "toffy nosed" and beyond them, wrongly imagined I think as Dorothy's mind was often in other places and she was trying to work out her future prospects. She liked to walk on her own and there are few roads and hedge-lined droves at Christchurch with which she was not familiar. Occasionally she made her way to the Sixteen Foot river half-a-mile distant and dangled her toes in the water, not a wise thing to do considering the Fen rivers harbour giant predatory pike and dreaded zander. Did Dorothy contemplate the making of these dead-straight waterways, hundreds of men spading clay from the river bed and building up embankments, then crowning them with roads? These were Scotch and Dutch prisoners-of-war forcibly marched to the Fens in 1650 and obliged to carry out the tasks. No self-respecting Fenmen would offer their hands to schemes which deprived them of their livelihoods. It would not surprise the writer if Dorothy had learned something about the epic history of the Fens and understood the spirit of the place. Occasionally her father went to the embankment to take her back to the rectory in time for one of those splendid meals.

Both Dorothy and her father had a high regard for Fen churches and they certainly visited some. Many were erected on specially constructed rafts, especially on siltland, and it is known that beneath some fanes streams actually flow around the foundations. Anything between five-hundred to eight-hundred years have passed and still these glorious old churches stand vertically erect. It was an incredulous thing to Henry Sayers and his daughter who were well read in these matters. *The Nine Tailors* admirably reflects the sheer magnificence of these churches, a few brought together in Fenchurch St. Paul. Dorothy's father would have cherished an appointment to the living of Walpole St. Peter or Terrington St. Clement, the latter church one of Dorothy's favourites. She was seen on more than one occasion admiring the double hammerbeam roof at St. Wendreda's church, March, taking note of the astonishing array of one-hundred-and-twenty angel figures, most half life-size, filling the air as it were with their pinions as they alightened on the hammerbeams.

After marriage, Dorothy and her husband occasionally visited Christchurch attired in leather outfits and wearing goggles as befits eager motorcyclists. It must have been a strange sight for the demure Henry Sayers and his wife when the bike, engine chattering, came to a halt on the gravelled driveway. Perhaps it went a little bit against the grain but whatever they thought was never disclosed. "At Whitsuntide Dorothy and Mac drove to Christchurch on a motorcycle and for the first time the Reverend and Mrs. Sayers met their son-in-law. The visit was a success. Dorothy reported to Ivy that they had three days of gorgeous weather and that she had taken her mother out on the motorcycle for a short run 'and she was ever so sporting – seemed thoroughly to enjoy going fast'." – (Barbara Reynolds: DOROTHY SAYERS, HER LIFE AND SOUL. Reproduced by permission of Hodder & Stoughton Limited).

Dorothy had scant regard for motor cars and preferred by far the incessant chatter of a motorcycle's engine beneath its rider and rush of wind around the ears and the sheer freedom of the road. Mac was quite taken up by his visits to the rectory, got on well with his wife's parents, and was quick to observe the meticulous running of the Sayers household. He was favourably impressed with the neatly-kept gardens.

During her visits to Christchurch Dorothy put in appearances at the church and enjoyed singing in the choir. She took her place in the chancel sporting her M.A. apparel and sang with gusto with her colleagues who, no doubt, felt a trifle subdued by the "Oxford presence". Her exhilarating walks in the countryside helped her mind to concentrate and sometimes she could be spotted in the rectory gardens walking contemplatively her mind immersed in thought, perhaps forming a plot for Lord Peter and conjuring up suitable titles for novels. When she returned to the rectory she ascended the grand staircase to her room and pressed pen vigorously to paper jotting down ideas before they abandoned her mind – a ritual employed by every author.

Every day at the rectory was a busy one. Mrs. Sayers arose quite early and had breakfast when many parishioners were already at work in the fields. Her husband quietly went about his tasks, making a break for a light lunch and eagerly anticipated the most splendid meal of all, dinner prepared to perfection. The Sayers employed a couple who carried out most of the chores. Hired help lived on site and their wages were a little more than could be earned on the land. It was an acceptable arrangement, most clergy employing a maid, a cook and a gardener.

During one of her summer visits Dorothy organised a garden party in aid of church funds. She gave one of her pretty dresses to a local lady to wear for the occasion. Dorothy wore a "fetching" dress and added humour to the event by walking about the rectory grounds sporting a wide-brimmed hat, her teeth clenching an empty pipe! Mixing with elite circles at London taught her one or two humorous tricks of the trade and she enjoyed the effect it had on the parishioners. She liked her rings and presented one to a Christchurch lady. Dorothy and Mac spent an enjoyable holiday at the rectory in 1927 and again visited the village a few months later.

Henry Sayers was a tired man. Always he endeavoured to fulfil his role as pastor faithfully, putting care and effort into whatever he did. He had not been in the best of health for several days and given to a troublesome cough but, as always, he continued to busy himself with parochial duties. Returning home one day he told his wife he was going to bed and it was there a short time later Mrs. Sayers found he had passed away. The family practitioner announced that his patient had been suffering from pneumonia. His passing was entirely unexpected and the parish, who regarded him as a true friend and wise counsellor, felt a deep sense of loss. The Reverend Sayers had held the living of Christchurch for eleven years.

Dorothy enjoyed a close bond with her parents who never failed to support and encourage her, especially in the years of doubt and indecision. After her husband's death, Mrs. Sayers had only a limited time at Christchurch rectory and Dorothy and Mac saw her settled at a house at Witham, Essex where she died just a few months after the Reverend Sayers demise. She was interred in his grave in the proximity of the chancel at Christchurch. For years the parishioners were perplexed that Dorothy never had a headstone set above the grave and it was only in recent years that a small inscribed plaque was placed above the grave by the Dorothy Sayers Society. It is said that the long absence of a memorial to her parents was an oversight by Dorothy who was constantly engaged in literary and associated work. The Society placed a commemorative plaque in Bluntisham rectory in 1981 but it was stolen. The plaque was replaced in 1993, the anniversary of Dorothy Sayers birth, and unveiled by Norma Major.

Dorothy's time in the Fens engraved upon her the unique geological achievement of that historically famous level. Her knowledge in this respect can be readily detected in *The Nine Tailors* which is generally acknowledged to be a tribute to the Fens and the stoic qualities of the Fen people. Dorothy felt thoroughly at home while writing it but the work had to be delayed while she prepared *Murder Must Advertise*, an entertaining novel but its celebrated author was not entirely happy with it. When at last she finally wrote finis to *The Nine Tailors* the novel was acclaimed a success and has run to more than thirty editions. A critic wrote "it is more than a detective story; it is a really good novel of astonishing virtuosity".

Himself a bellringer, the writer regards *The Nine Tailors* as the finest work ever to advertise the attractions of the art and its ancient traditions among such a huge readership of non-ringers. *The Nine Tailors* exemplifies the master stroke of Dorothy Sayers feeling for traditional values. It revolves around a fascinating craft, an exact science, and to a useful extent the novel attempts to unravel the mysteries of bellringing and delightfully introduces the complexities of the art and expounds the unquestioned devotedness of its disciples. In its pages is sensed the epic struggles of the Fen people when floods threatened farms and villages. Arguably it is the best filip to the strengths and attractions of bellringing ever produced because it is so unusual. Therein lies the strength of *The Nine Tailors*. Hidden away in the story are visions of the England we love.

One does not live in the solitary landscape without absorbing something from its past. Dorothy Sayers may have intimated that she did not care for the Fens but in *The Nine Tailors*, "one of the cunningest and most engaging detective stories ever read" there is a different point of view regarding the land of the three quarter sky. The story is no less a monument to her obvious knowledge of the Fens, its people and their unique characteristics which she dutifully engraved upon her mind. By all accounts the Great Level did fascinate her, as certainly did the magnificent churches, soaring steeples and sonorous bells and the men and women that love to ring them.

Whether or not Dorothy realised it, with the help of Lord Peter, the Reverend and Mrs. Venables, ringers Wally Pratt, Hezekiah Lavender, Jack Godfrey and the rest – oh! and Tailor Paul, Fenchurch's noble tenor bell and its metallic companions – murderers all – she eulogised the Fens and the art of bellringing better than any other. And for good measure gave Bluntisham and Christchurch a nice slice of fame.

Reverend Henry Sayers, M.A. held the living at Christchurch for eleven years. The memorial stone on the grave of Mr. and Mrs. Sayers was placed there by the Dorothy L. Sayers Society.

IN MEMORIAM
REVD HENRY SAYERS M.A.
1854 – 1928
AND
HELEN MARY SAYERS
1856 – 1929

Henry Sayers exchanged livings for Christchurch rectory where he died.
The Victorian church nearby had a tower which became unstable.
Privately owned, the old rectory is smaller than that at Bluntisham.
It was at Christchurch that Dorothy Sayers completed one of her novels.

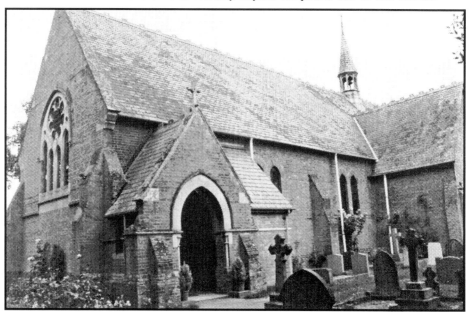

The attractive mediaeval church at Bluntisham has a unique
chancel. Here, the Sayers family attended services, walking from the
rectory, some distance away.

Dorothy walked to the village shop along this road at Christchurch.
Entrances to the parish church and rectory are on the left.
Below: Church interior at Christchurch. Occasionally Dorothy sang in
the choir attired in her Oxford apparel

Above: the solitary wind-swept Fens. Below: Terrington St. Clement, not dissimilar to a priory church, one of three local fanes which inspired Dorothy Sayers for her internationally acclaimed novel The Nine Tailors.

Dorothy Sayers was a frequent visitor to St. Peter's church, Upwell.
She taught French part-time at Upwell's mediaeval rectory below.

THE NINE TAILORS

The Nine Tailors is an acknowledged literary masterpiece. Many consider it Dorothy Sayers finest novel, much more than an ordinary detective story. The author herself regarded the work as a labour of love and in that sentiment one glimpses a hidden fascination for the Fens. The book embodies her love and respect for her father and charmingly portrays a man of the cloth drawn spiritually and physically to the Perpendicular attractions of the Fens' magnificent old churches. In its earlier pages is sensed the character of the flatlands and the stoic qualities of the hardy people that live and work there.

The plot entwines with and weaves into a rich era in rural terms second to none in the annals of England's historic past. Dorothy recalled the times spent with her parents in the Fens. The novel clearly identifies with a landscape of wide horizons and it is entirely appropriate that the mortal remains of the couple rest in the soil where water was wont to roam. It may even be said that the work is, in a non-explicit way, a monument to them. For bellringers *The Nine Tailors* identifies with their language and art as does the bible with clergy folk. It is saturated with enthusiasm for the art. Dorothy weaved the mystery of the plot with bellringing so convincingly as to convince the least infatuated reader that Fenchurch St. Paul at the centre of the story does actually exist.

Her father shines through the pages as the Reverend Theodore Venables, happily married to his caring, concerned wife – and to the bells. A true enough situation in many bellringing households! Comfortably installed in the old rectory overshadowed by the great church of St. Paul, tower rising above the solitary landscape as do many noble Fen sentinels. Gathered around a blazing fire in the middle of winter, and savouring dripping teacakes and muffins and sipping cups of tea. How often did that happen within the cosy confines of Christchurch rectory? Theodore is a bellringer and by sheer fine chance realises that his unexpected visitor Lord Peter can pull a good rope, too. On one or two occasions in the story Dorothy diverts from facts as bellringers know them. It is not allowed for ringers engaged in ringing peals or smaller numbers of changes to hand their ropes to others. It simply is not safe to do so. In any case individuals engaged in ringing more than five thousand changes which constitutes a recognised peal, putting up with sweating periods, persperation dripping from foreheads onto the nose and onto the torso, as well as tolerating one or two broken blood blisters between fingers, rightly feel a profound sense of achievement as they sink thankfully onto seats at the successful conclusion of a three-hour peal. That is the sport of the bellringing game and there is no half time. Needless to say smaller "touches" are more popular and give an even greater sense of pleasure to ringers, especially when performed well.

Dorothy Sayers sense of infinity with Gothic buildings matured in the Fens, developing from her visits to local churches. One imagines her questioning mind enraptured at the soaring steeples at, for instance, Leverington and Whittlesey the latter impressing beholders with proportional grandeur. She envisaged a typical Fen village with two or three straight roads, usually a crossroad encompassed by a patchwork pattern of virilent fields intersected by arrow-like drains and embankments. A community of farms, the inevitable smithy and a pub or two and plain cottages with back gardens yielding a mixture of vegetables and flowers. Rising above it all, surrounded by gnarled, ivy-covered trees, the ancient fane enriched with every conceivable nicety of mediaeval adornment, ugly gargoyles, cherubims, huge glowing windows, a forest of pillars and the pièce de résistance, the angel host aloft in the ceiling seemingly fluttering across the gap and alighting on the hammerbeams. The most splendid external sight observable from a good ten miles away ranged against a full sky a tower of woundrous beauty tantalisingly beckoning modernday pilgrims. Such is the visual reward of the Fens.

Dorothy's fictitious place name Fenchurch St. Paul, embodies the existing name Christchurch. She was familiar with several fen villages in the vicinity of Wisbech, King's Lynn and March. Dorothy invented place-names for *The Nine Tailors*, for instance Walbeach, a combination of Wisbech and Walpole or Walsoken. Less than ten miles from Christchurch stands the classical church of Walpole St. Peter, one of the finest, though not largest of Perpendicular churches in the country, much visited and admired by members of the Royal family. The high altar is elevated to such a degree as to allow a vaulted passageway beneath. "The Queen of the Marsh" is a highly satisfying church and its survival all the more remarkable when considering that the surrounding silt land was frequently inundated and, of course, the church, too. The tower is all that remains of the earlier building which had to be pulled down, foundations badly weakened by repeated washing. Henry Sayers surely visited Walpole, and his daughter if she had never seen the church must have heard about it.

In her commendable biography of Dorothy Sayers, Dr. Barbara Reynolds mentions that three Fen churches inspired the invention of Fenchurch St. Paul. Terrington St. Clement, Upwell St. Peter and the ancient pilgrimage chapel of March St. Wendreda. It is feasible that Dorothy linked Terrington St. Clement with the known history of Marshland and the terrible floods which occurred in that region in centuries past. Early in the 17th century the spuming brine in its fury inundated Terrington not for the first time. The huge bulk of the 15th century tower was opened to accommodate parishioners driven from their homes by water incursion. There are a number of ancient flood towers in Marshland including those at West Walton and Tydd St. Giles, both separated from their respective church buildings.

If Walpole St. Peter's church is "Queen" then certainly neighbouring Terrington St. Clement is King. Dorothy was surely in awe of the granduer and dignity of St. Clement's for it resembles nothing less than a miniature cathedral. There is a wealth of pinnacles and the interior is saturated with light from more than eighty windows. To counteract possible movement a few inches separates the tower from the church, a precautionary measure should it begin to lean from the verticle. Terrington St. Clements, a 14th century gem, stands like an abbey. The writer is not surprised that Dorothy Sayers discovered inspiration here for her Fenchurch St. Paul.

St. Peter's church at Upwell also played a part in the design. The edifice engraved itself on Dorothy's perceptive mind on several occasions while teaching French at the mediaeval rectory, a stone's throw away. Essentially Perpendicular and wholly unlike Terrington, St. Peter's has a large range of square-headed windows and an octagon surmounts the 13th century tower. Gardens dividing the churchyard from the rectory grounds were once protected by a mediaeval defensive wall, but only a couple of turrets remain. Dorothy passed between these red-brick bastions, a rare feature not lost to her powers of observation. Something about St. Peter's church commanded her interest and she was sufficiently impressed to mention it in her notes.

St. Wendreda's church at March is entirely different to the others. Formerly a pilgrimage chapel it was heavily restored between 1340 and 1346 and contained the relic of St. Wendreda who had lived at March in the late 7th century. The church has a distinctive steeple with an unusual passageway and there are many interesting features. The Sayers family lived only five miles away and St. Wendreda's was a must for Dorothy's and her father's instinctive appreciation for grand old churches. Sir John Betjeman, late Poet Laureate, wrote that it was worth cycling forty miles in headwind to see St. Wendreda's church. One hardly thinks that Dorothy made the journey in that manner. She may have used a motorbike!

The church certainly impressed and the magnificent double-hammerbeam angel roof enthralled her. So much so she mentions it in *The Nine Tailors,* Mrs. Venables, proudly showing Lord Peter around Fenchurch St. Paul, says she thought the Fenchurch roof was even better than those at March or Needham Market! It should be pointed out that the roof at the latter place is not the double hammerbeam type.

A verger at St. Wendreda's church who taught the writer to handle bells told him he had once met Dorothy Sayers inside the church where she sat reflectively in a pew and studied the roof for a long time, jotting down notes.

These, then, are the three churches which Dorothy herself intimated served to inspire her to write *The Nine Tailors*. The writer is inclined to believe that a fourth church indirectly played a role in planning the novel. St. Botolph's church, Boston, in Lincolnshire, affectionately known as "The Stump", has an incredibly lofty tower crowned with a beautiful octagon. It does have an uncanny similarity to the design of the imaginary Fenchurch St. Paul printed in the novel.

Dorothy wanted an illustration of her fictitious fane to grace the work and she engaged an amateur architect, W. H. Redhead, to design it. The illustration depicts a great Perpendicular church with a splendid tower astonishingly like that at Boston but without the octagon. Twin windows of St. Botolph's tower's middle stage are reproduced in the illustration and serve as belfry windows while the latter are removed to the middle stage. Several other details are very similar to Boston's gorgeous and famous church.

To get anywhere in the Fens it is inevitable that travellers will occasionally find themselves en route via embankments used as hard roads. Twenty or thirty feet below on one side are fields and on the opposite side an almost sheer drop to the river. The Sixteen Foot drain is the nearest waterway to Christchurch and Dorothy and her parents had no choice but use the embankment road when journeying to Wisbech, Ely or March. Like the churches, Fen rivers are a notable feature of the landscape. Flanking the drains, fields produce a variety of super crops and green, brown and gold are dominant colours.

In times of drought the land becomes so dry as to produce a phenomenon unique to the Fens and known as the Fen Blow. Dorothy may well have seen fine soil whipped up by gusts of wind carried in a dense sand-like mass over the land, into neighbouring fields and into the backyards of villages and towns. Dorothy knew of this phenomenon which can occur in summer when drivers of vehicles passing through the swirling dust are obliged to switch on their lights.

The rivers mentioned in *The Nine Tailors* are fictitious. The Thirty Foot, for instance, reflects the tendency long ago to name new cuts after a form of measurement between the river banks. Previously the rivers or cuts as any true Fenman will recognise, were named after individuals who either had a part in their making or who was a person of influence. Thurlow's Drain is now the Sixteen Foot which Dorothy Sayers was familiar with. Mr. Thurlow was Oliver Cromwell's right-hand man in affairs of State and occupied a splendid house on the site of Wisbech Castle. The Forty Foot river which passes near Chatteris and joins the Sixteen Foot originally honoured Sir Cornelius Vermuyden, the architect of the scheme to drain the vast level. Serious drainage commenced in 1630 and was not successfully completed until 1850 with the drainage of Whittlesey Mere. The Sixteen Foot river is indirectly linked, as are many drains, with the massive Fen guardians at Wiggenhall St. Germans. There are four massive pump units capable of discharging more than 6,000,000 tonnes of water over a twenty-four hour continuous working period.

Another phenomenon Dorothy may have noticed in the Fens is this: according to the strength of the breeze bells may be heard ringing at distances of as much as twelve miles. The writer has listened to the octave of St. Mary's church, Whittlesey, from the lofty parapets of St. Wendreda's church tower. Also the bells of Wisbech St. Mary and Upwell St. Peter have been heard at March on a still evening drifting over the Fens at distances of eight miles, just as they did in days gone by warning travellers in the hazardous fens to seek the safety of higher ground before darkness fell.

It was written that names appearing in *The Nine Tailors* are fictitious. Some however derive from surnames surviving to this day in the Fens. Gotobed and Thoday can be found in the area and Wilderspin is linked with Chatteris, not far away from Christchurch. *The Nine Tailors* is very different from Dorothy Sayers other novels although they all share Lord Peter Wimsey. The story contributed a whole new challenge to her literary prowess and the Fens can be thankful for that. It introduces the science of ringing bells. The story emerged from her bones so to speak, her soul saturated with refined knowledge of the English lowlands. The so-called "desolate" landscape described thus by various other authors, wrongly so in the writer's opinion, has a way of captivating the soul and it shows in Dorothy's entertaining book of country social life. Her sense of perceptiveness in a defined geological level is refreshingly observable in *The Nine Tailors.*

She may not have felt over enthusiasitic about the land of wide horizons but in planning and writing the book she admitted the work was a labour of love. Love of the memories of her time spent in the Fens? Love of her parents who spent several years in the area? Love of the magnificent churches built as foils against the sombre flatness, soaring towers giving richly detailed relief against the distant, treeless horizon where the sky merges with the earth?

It was to the churches that old-time Fenmen and their families resorted after a day of back-breaking toil, wrestling with newly drained soil, tending to flocks and herds grazing on the salt marsh. Dearbought land it was rightly named, seized from the sea which bided its time then roared back with a vengeance. Dorothy familiarised herself with the Fens' epic history. Her studies impelled her into a story which, despite her obvious satisfaction in writing it, initially convinced her, wrongly as it turned out, that it would not stimulate enough interest to make it viable. Fen Slodgers of olden times are mirrored in the farm workers portraying recognised stoic qualities handed down to later generations and Dorothy appreciated that. She worked them into the plot and embroidered their quiet, strong, immovable attitudes into *The Nine Tailors.* They are present in the characters of Ezra Wilderspin, Hezekiah Lavendar and Jack Godfrey, men of metal happily taking up their positions in the circle of bellropes, and, of course, the campanological enthusiast Reverend Theodore Venables, the epitome of Dorothy's father.

These and other characters we can well imagine lived at Fenchurch St. Paul. There are people like them in the Fens. Readers of *The Nine Tailors* can be excused for believing that Fenchurch St. Paul really does exist and that visitors awheel along the embankment river system will expect to see in the distance the massive bell tower envisaged by its author. The architect of the fictitious church presented Dorothy with a design based on her own ideas of what it should look like. The church reflects an anagram of Dorothy's much admired Fen churches, Terrington St. Clement, Upwell St. Peter and March St. Wendreda. I wonder whether Boston and Walpole St. Peter churches came into it? They deserved to.

In her zeal to understand the Fens' history, Dorothy captured the trauma of the urgent hour which Fen dwellers had to contend with when floods threatened their acres, homes and livelihood. Water rising perceptibly against embankments, the sheer weight of it pressing against hard packed soil, exploring fissures and expanding cavities, rooting out weak spots, then whoosh! a section explodes and disappears in a spuming flurry of hissing water. It pours through the breach and establishes a hold on the marginal lowland, transforming deep furrows into channels, overcoming the fields, uprooting young trees, demolishing farm buildings and entering farmsteads. A few hours later the evening light sparkles on a wilderness of strange calm, a great ocean as far as the eye can see deep enough to drown a man. Cattle and sheep float grotesquely, legs upraised and, at the breach, the water having spent its force is reduced to a trickle.

In the story Theodore Venables, expecting the worst, prepares his parishioners for impending disaster. Mindful of Fenland's embattled past, Dorothy Sayers introduces a glimmer of the trauma which took place in these parts. In more recent years the Fenmen, girded to action, filled thousands of sandbags in attempts to stem the water, even dropping army tanks into the breaches, anything to resist the flow. Fenmen have seen it all before and Dorothy Sayers knew that nothing would ever induce them to give up. Such is their spirit, inbred from their water-borne ancestry and akin to the Battle of Britain. She hints of man's greatest conception to save the Fens – two great Bedford rivers cut in 1631 and 1650 respectively. In between them is lush grassland stretching more than twenty miles, grazing meadows varying from almost half-a-mile to three-quarters of a mile wide.

In winter, cattle, sheep and horses are removed to safe harbours and in the event of heavy rain and snow the rivers swell and overflow onto the washland which acts as a safety valve, water covering it as far as the eye can see. The warm colours of sunrise and sunset reflect on water and create pastel hues stretching from the distant horizon to one's feet. An awe inspiring sight to behold, especially when wild geese from Iceland and swans from Russia migrate to the level. Dorothy had this in mind when she wrote *The Nine Tailors*.

There is much inspiration from the Fens and the book's author absorbed a goodly amount as background material for the project. She was also inspired by another book The Nebuly Coat written soon after the turn of the last century. It was set around marshland which surrounded a great church protected by seabanks. Here, in part, the Terrington connection is seen.

One supposes that with her intrinsic insight of the importance of old churches and as master of plots sooner or later Dorothy would invent a church, introduce a body and an unusual slant into unnatural death. No record testifies that an individual was ever done to death by the sound of bells at unbearably close proximity. Certainly to stand in a belfry for more than a few minutes when the bells are ringing is not advisable. To be tied up and lodged beneath the swinging monsters while the perspiring team below engaged in ringing a lengthy peal of 15,000–odd changes over a period of nine hours non–stop ringing is an unspeakable, mind–boggling thing. Bellringing is a peculiar art to Britain and a few countries of Commonwealth origin where the English went to live taking their craft with them. By their powerful and sonorous sounds – some call it a cacophony – bells relate emotionally with the past. Wherever the English went in the world, among several things they remember is the sound of bells drifting in the evening air above the green countryside. It is a nostalgic sound heard in hills and valleys, cities, towns and villages, mountains and the flatlands. Like them or not, bells pealed in the traditional English manner are synonymous with our heritage, as English as football and cricket. They are very much part of our splendid Gothic heritage. Dorothy's father derived much satisfaction and inspiration from the free–flowing movement of overhead vaulting, soaring arches, geometrical windows and pinnacles and towers thrusting skywards. These are sights to behold in Britain and bells, confined and unseen in thousands of towers which dot the countryside, make their presence known in cascades of changes which the English lovingly nurtured into a science.

Perpendicular refinement portrayed in timber and stone was a prerequisite of Henry Sayers faith, the sweetness of biblical expression in the liturgical sense was as salt to enhance the savoury content of a good meal. His zeal mantled his family and the moulding of his daughter's earliest memories entwined with her father's appreciation of these things. They went with her to Oxford which one might realise is the birthplace of middle and late Gothic. In goodly measure the Gothic principle entered the energetic mind of Dorothy Sayers and was moulded in goodly measure in some of her literary works, especially *The Nine Tailors*. How well she perceived the stately conception of mediaeval designers and craftsmen in their works at Terrington St. Clement, Upwell and March and seen to brilliant effect at many other ennobled edifices in the Fens.

31

KENT TREBLE BOB AND ALL THAT

Dorothy Sayers admiration for structural Gothic masterpieces led her to discover the secular/spiritual purposes of bells. In turn this led her to the mid–tower, gallery and ground floor areas where bellringers practice their craft. There she met the men and women, aptly named silver tongued mathematicians, mostly rural folk of modest achievement, artistes in metallic sounds more English than the rose.

Dorothy never handled a bell which is not as easy as it looks. A long standing campanologist, the writer expresses surprise at this as she was, in the general pursuit of literary ambitions, quite prepared to try anything. That she watched bells being rung is unquestionable but she may have found the physical side of ringing bells daunting and no doubt had heard a few tales from enthusiasts that the unwary ringer might easily be pulled upwards if the wooden stay on the bell's headstock snaps in half because the rope had been pulled too hard and not checked, the bell turning right over, coiling up the rope on the wheel in the process. A frightening experience but there's a different aspect to the picture in every pursuit. If it's done correctly there is nothing to fear. Dorothy preferred to employ her analytical mind in endeavouring to understand how ringers sort their way in complex fashion through the mass of figures, mainly paperwork in "pricking" out changes. This can be learned from numerous technical books but putting the knowledge to the test by actually ringing the changes together as a team is quite another thing.

Skilled ringers memorise the "blue line", a wriggly mark depicting the path of any particular bell in the work which is called "method". The blue line, with or without rows of figures is to bellringers what quavers are to musicians. A more advanced ringer is able to merely glance at the blue line, a diagram actually, and then ring it with other ringers, carrying in his or her head and performing the piece in row–upon–row of half–pull non–repetitional changes. Stamina and a dedicated amount of concentration and a fine sense of rhythm is essential as well as the ability to gauge distances accurately as some bells are smaller than others and swing quickly whereas the big ones revolve at a slower pace. Bells thrust and plunge in their pits, every movement transmitted through ropes varying from thirty feet to as much as ninety feet in length. Ringers make instinctive decisions to brake or check the bells' movements in their onrush or give them their head. Instinct commonly known as "ropesight", a sense of knowing which ringer or rope to follow in the space of a split–second combines with physical impetus depending on the weight of the bells becomes the driving force, the soul of bellringing, meticulously applying the method or pattern in the ringers' minds into split–second action. It is superb exercise both mentally and physically.

Dorothy produced reams of paperwork about bells and the ringing of them and she noted their fascinating inscriptions which play an important part in the antiquity of the subject. Her most assiduous studies were devoted to familiarising herself with the "method", the straight lines and wriggly bits, coursing orders and intricate compositions and the conducting of them in "touches" and peals. This particularly related to Kent Treble Bob which, no doubt, was recommended to her as a fine musical method. She had a nose for secondhand book shops and curiosity led to her acquiring a book about change ringing. With the help of mentors she struggled to understand the "blue line" until she could memorise it, just as bellringers do. This aspect of the art fascinated her and it undoubtedly played a major role in the writing of *The Nine Tailors.* Knowledge of method ringing does not come easily and for Dorothy it was a challenge. Her mentors explained the ins and outs (a bellringing term) of the work and how the "blue line" applied to all methods classified as Plain, Delight, Surprise and Principle.

The pattern can be simple or complex and is woven by each of the team into the sequence of changes which might be a "touch" of a few minutes' duration or a full peal of more than 5,000 changes requiring in the region of three hours continuous ringing. Someone conducts and at certain periods in the ringing calls either a "bob" or a "single", these affecting the coursing order of the work, thus avoiding repetition.

All this was a whole new aspect to Dorothy Sayers and she sensed the uniqueness of working into the text of her novel a living art so much a part of English social life. It was a vibrant essence of the countryside and Dorothy's experiences of the Fens would form the essential background to the story. Even so, she entertained doubts about it but, as she intimated it was, after all, a labour of love. The *Oxford Companion of Music* described the novel as being of peculiar interest to readers as it offered an explanation of changeringing which is generally acknowledged as something of a mystery to most people. *The Nine Tailors* is described as a story enriched with special knowledge. If Dorothy had learned to handle bells her insight of the art of change ringing would have been enhanced. Being a non-ringer she did surprisingly well and while acknowledging her novel does contain a few technical errors, the fact that it was very favourably received by the bellringing fraternity and acclaimed by general readers, in her own words, made her "sinfully proud".

Kent Treble Bob, the method employed in the *The Nine Tailors,* was popular among bellringers countrywide during the 1920's and 1930's. The method was rated as the most musical among several Treble Bob variations and the Reverend Theodore Venable's remark as to its popularity and unbeatable musical qualities do bear weight. Having been weaned on Oxford and Kent Treble Bob the writer concurs with those sentiments but he would be considered out of touch nowadays. Some methods are threaded with mind blowing complexity and not all are noted for musical qualities but are challenging to ringers for reason of their yearning to achieve something very difficult. Numerous Everests exist in the fields of campanology and one has only to scan the weekly peal reports in *The Ringng World* to realise the art's popularity.

The Central Council of Church Bellringers was so impressed it offered Dorothy a vice-presidency but she declined, being greatly involved in many other things. *The Nine Tailors* extols the art of bellringing in a socially friendly light and the art's disciples, at the very least, are right in acknowledging her efforts as laudable. No other book or article has done for bellringing among the rank and file of non-participants as that written by Dorothy L. Sayers.

She entered into the grimy, fume-laden world of bell founders and connected the fictitious bells of Fenchurch St. Paul with a mediaeval bellfounder at King's Lynn. She had every reason to be proud of her voluntary association with the noble art. Her engrossment with bellringing and sense of enthusiasm with the men and women that ring bells was for her an enjoyable exercise combining science with tradition. It was a dramatic approach in the preparation of a novel which in style and content can be described as a world beater. The first edition was published in 1934 and by 1954 twenty-two editions had rolled off the press, with no less than three reprints in one year. More editions replenished book shelves in 1959 and again in 1962, 1965, 1969 and 1972. Other editions appeared since the latter mentioned year.

In *The Nine Tailors* the mystery evolves around bells and bellringers. The bells of Fenchurch St. Paul rang to a record-breaking length of changes and, as they clamoured, a man bound hand and foot a few feet beneath them dies a terrifying death, his brain battered by the endless din. The writer knows of no-one having suffered to this extent at such close quarters. It is said that if someone was accidently locked in a belfry and the bells rang for an undeterminable time they might well die. Certainly their hearing would be permanently impaired and it is likely they would be driven mad.

Dorothy was fascinated by bellringers' language. As in practically every sport mysterious words apply, quite unfamiliar to the uninitiated. Almost every city and town and a lot of villages, too, have a campanological method named after them, for instance the town of March has a method "March Delight" named after it. Even stars in the heavens are honoured in this way. Dorothy Sayers in her novel mentions Grandsire Major, a relatively simple method. Theodore Venables in his praise of Kent Treble Bob Major politely dismisses Grandsire Major as lacking certain music compared to Kent. It's surprising that Dorothy chose Kent rather than Oxford Treble Bob for her novel when considering she spent a few years in the city of domes and spires. Presumably she was ruled by her mentors who, one supposes, extolled the musical merits of Kent Treble Bob, a kinder method to ringers in the physical sense and that Oxford Treble Bob deployed a trap for the unwary.

A SHORT HISTORY OF KENT TREBLE BOB

Oxford and Kent Treble Bob were early pioneers in the fields of change-ringing for many years dominated by Plain Bob and Grandsire which were always recognised as orthodox methods. Many so-called methods composed in the seventeenth century were published by Fabian Stedman, a Cambridge printer and a bellringer at St. Benet's church, Cambridge. These methods bore strange names, i.e. The Whirligigge, My Honey, Camelion, and despite their antiquity most would not be recognised in present times.

Treble Bob methods abound but the two popularly practised in the nineteenth century and early twentieth century were Oxford and Kent Treble Bob, identical in almost every respect. Oxford is the oldest of the two and the Kent verson was published under the title New Treble Bob and took a long time to catch on. Mr. Shipway was the first to give it the name of Kent Treble Bob and it eventually became more popular with bellringers and was extensively practised.

Kent Treble Bob has always been recognised as musical. The general rule in ringing it is to keep the tenors together thus rendering a pleasing musical effect. Easier place-making reduces physical effort to some extent, Oxford having a "thirds" place coursing down then requiring abrupt change of direction and working out again. This is a trap for the unwary and, if it is not not carefully observed, potentially destructive to the piece being rung.

The earliest peal (5,120 changes) recorded of Oxford Treble Bob was achieved by the Society of Union Scholars on December 27th, 1718. It was customary for ringers to call the method after their own title, in this instance "Union Treble Bob". A variation of this method, 8,448 changes composed by J. Reeves was noted by Mr. Shipway: "This peal was rung in the Kent variation of Treble Bob by the Society of Junior Cumberlands in 1787 at St. Mary's, Whitechapel, being the first time it was ever performed". No written record of the peal exists but since Mr. Shipway took part it is regarded as authentic.

Several peals of Union Treble Bob were recorded by the College Youths and other societies, some peal ringers recognising the method as Oxford Treble Bob. The peal of 5,120 changes was entered in a peal book by the Union Scholars and later presented to the British Museum. Jasper Whitfield Snowdon wrote that the peal was true in its composition "perhaps owing more to good luck than good management, as it was probably only considered true from the fact that the treble lead-ends were true".

In 1768 the tendency of Treble Bob peals to be false when the treble dodged before, came to the notice of those ringing them. "The rumour of this discovery soon spread a general alarm throughout the whole art scarcely a peal being rung but its truth was now suspected. Indeed, many ringers' fears were but too well founded, for on a strict investigation of the peals then rung, the old peal above-mentioned (5,120) excepted, two out of three were absolutely false".

It is doubtful that Dorothy Sayers grappled with the complexities of false changes in pursuing the coursing order of Kent Treble Bob. *The Nine Tailors* attempt rang true!